Poetic Meditations for Successful Living

David L. Ballinger

Proverbs 3:5+6

PublishAmerica
Baltimore

© 2011 by David L. Ballinger
All rights reserved. No part of this book may be reproduced, stored in a retrieval system or transmitted in any form or by any means without the prior written permission of the publishers, except by a reviewer who may quote brief passages in a review to be printed in a newspaper, magazine or journal.

First printing

PublishAmerica has allowed this work to remain exactly as the author intended, verbatim, without editorial input.

Hardcover 978-1-4560-9172-9
Softcover 978-1-4560-9173-6
PUBLISHED BY PUBLISHAMERICA, LLLP
www.publishamerica.com
Baltimore

Printed in the United States of America

Acknowledgements

When I preached a sermon series through the Ten Commandments, I used many resources. The most outstanding was a book titled, *God's Blueprint for Living, New Perspectives on the Ten Commandments* by Dr. David A. Seamands. He was also my professor of pastoral care and counseling at Asbury Theological Seminary. Many of the poetic reflections came from my pondering the teaching, stories, images and phrases in this excellent book.

Other resources which influenced my meditations were *The Wesley Bible* (A Personal Study Bible for Holy Living); the writings of John R. W. Stott, Henrietta C. Mears, Martin Luther, E. Stanley Jones and many others.

My thanks to Dr. Don Joy, my friend, mentor, and Professor of Christian Education and Human Development at Asbury Theological Seminary, for allowing me to process with him my own struggles in applying the Law and the Gospel to my own life.

My thanks to my beautiful wife, Laura, for her love and encouragement; to my three kids, Brian, Stacey and Brett for making life exciting and fun; to my Mom, brothers, sister, in–laws, nieces and nephews: You make life fun, too; and to Trinity United Methodist Church in Huntington, Indiana: Thanks that we can live out the Christian life in the context of community.

David L. Ballinger

Preface

I started writing poems on a regular basis for my wife for her birthday and on Valentine's Day. I wrote them not because I was a good poet, but because I was too cheap to buy a card for five dollars. The sayings and poems in the cards were nice, but too impersonal and too expensive. My wife liked the poems written to her because they were more personal, meaningful, and sometimes, funny.

Then I thought, if my wife, Laura, likes my poems, maybe God would like them as well. I preached a sermon series on the Ten Commandments. I thought a lot about the relationship between God's Law and God's Gospel. In my ponderings, I felt a sense of the Spirit's leadings in these poetic reflections. I wrote them for God with the hope that a few people might read them, and learn and ponder. I hope God likes them and I hope you enjoy them also.

David L. Ballinger

Table of Contents

The Greatest Commandment of All............ 11
The Greatest Commandment 12

Show Us the Father............................... 13
What is God Like? 14

The Ten Commandments....................... 16
The Ten Commandments Poem.................17

The First Commandment....................... 20
The 1st Commandment Poem 21
False Gods..23
Two Masters..25
Lower Left-Hand Corner.............................26
Therefore...27

The Second Commandment................... 28
Who or What is Your God? 29
What is Idolatry? 30
Commandments 1 & 2................................31
Who He Really is...32
Jealous? 34
I Am 35
The Only True Picture of God 37

The Third Commandment 38
Audience Chamber 39
Oaths 41
God's Last Name 42
In My Name 43
Uncouth 45

The Fourth Commandment 46
Sunday 47
Sabbath Time 49

The Fifth Commandment 50
Honor 51
Never Cross a Child 52
Who's The Boss? 54

The Sixth Commandment 56
Murder 57
Do Kill Your Enemy (This Way) 60
God's Image 61
Life and Death 62

The Seventh Commandment 65
Sexuality 66
Shy 69
The 7th Commandment Poem 71
Strict 72
Moral Fences 74
Sex Advice for Husband and Wife 76
Happy Marriage 78
Wow! 79

The Eighth Commandment 80
The 8th Commandment Poem 81
Dignity 82
Thief 83

The Ninth Commandment 84
The Ways We Lie 85
The Cure for Lying 86
Sorry Mom for Lying 87
The Truth and a Lie 88
Court Justice 89
The Human Heart 90
Words 91
Reputation 92
Respectable Christians 93
The Living Lie 94
God Can and Can't 96
Ain't 97
Fly Catcher 98
Ouch 99

The Tenth Commandment 101
Covetousness 102
The Tenth Commandment Poem 104

Law and Gospel 105
Grace and Truth 106
Law and Gospel 107
God's Offer 108
The Purpose of God's Law 109
The Cross as a Tree 110
Four Limericks on Law and Grace 111

Exodus and John..........112
Exodus..........113
Two Mountains..........114
Moses..........115
Mount Sinai..........116
The Ten Commandments..........117
Decalogue..........118

The Trinitarian Blessing..........119
The Trinity..........120

God's Will..........122
My Will and God's Will..........123
Sorry, Thank you, Please..........124

The Greatest Commandment of All

One of them, an expert in the law, tested him with this question: "Teacher, which is the greatest commandment in the Law?"
Jesus replied: "'Love the Lord your God with all your heart and with all your soul and with all your mind.' This is the first and greatest commandment. And the second is like it: 'Love your neighbor as yourself.' All the law and the prophets hang on these two commandments" (Matthew 22:35-40 NIV).

The Greatest Commandment

Once asked an expert in the Law,
What is the greatest commandment of all?
Jesus replied…
Love the Lord with all of your heart.
This is the first place we must start.
Love the Lord with all your soul.
This is what will make us whole.
Love the Lord with all your mind.
This will make us wise and kind.
God's Spirit will in us initiate,
With faith, the Father, we will imitate.
God's Spirit is poured out from above.
We receive Him and manifest His love.

Show Us the Father

Jesus answered, "I am the way and the truth and the life. No one comes to the Father except through me. If you really knew me, you would know my Father as well. From now on, you do know him and have seen him."

Philip said, "Lord, show us the Father; that will be enough for us."

Jesus answered, "Don't you know me, Philip, even after I have been among you such a long time? Anyone who has seen me has seen the Father" (John 14:6-9 NIV).

What is God Like?

Philip said, Show us the Father.
Jesus said, What do you mean?
Have I been with you so long, Philip,
And the Father you haven't seen?

What is God like, disciple?
Oh, can't you even tell?
Is He a one-eyed monster
Who wants to throw us into hell?

Is He a doting grandfather,
With a white and flowing beard,
Who is very nice and senile,
But is really kind of weird?

Is God a big policeman,
Who's always on patrol,
Who can't wait to catch us,
And make us pay the toll?

A perfectionistic mother?
"Oh, that's not good enough.
If I am ever to love you,
You'll have to improve your stuff."

Is He an unmoved mover
Who wound up the universe,
And now sits way off yonder
Distant, cold and terse?

Is God big, mean and scary,
Who frightens us to tears?
Or is this a projection
Of our sins and guilty fears?

Oh, Jesus, show us the Father,
Is he really odd?
He's not at all, says Jesus.
He is a Christ-like God.

The Ten Commandments

I. I am the Lord your God, who brought you out of the land of Egypt, out of the house of bondage. You shall have no other gods before Me.
II. You shall not make yourself a carved image, or any likeness of anything that is in heaven above, or that is in the earth beneath, or that is in the water under the earth; you shall not bow down to them nor serve them. For I, the LORD your God, am a jealous God, visiting the iniquity of the fathers on the children to the third and fourth generations of those who hate Me, but showing mercy to thousands, to those who love Me and keep My commandments.
III. You shall not take the name of the LORD your God in vain, for the LORD will not hold him guiltless who takes His name in vain.
IV. Remember the Sabbath day, to keep it holy. Six days you shall labor and do all your work, but the seventh day is the Sabbath of the Lord your God. In it you shall do no work: you, nor your son, nor your daughter, nor your male servant, nor your female servant, nor your cattle, nor your stranger who is within your gates. For in six days the LORD made the heavens and the earth, the sea, and all that is in them, and rested the seventh day. Therefore the LORD blessed the Sabbath day and hallowed it.
V. Honor your father and your mother, that your days may be long upon the land which the LORD your God is giving you.
VI. You shall not murder.
VII. You shall not commit adultery.
VIII. You shall not steal.
IX. You shall not bear false witness against your neighbor.
X. You shall not covet your neighbor's house; you shall not covet your neighbor's wife, nor his male servant, nor his female servant, nor his ox, nor his donkey, nor anything that is your neighbor's (Exodus 20:2-17 NKJV).

The Ten Commandments Poem

God's great Ten Commandments
Begin with saving grace.
As He powerfully delivered His people
Out of that bondage place.

The first commandment has to do
With whom He is, the Lord.
He is the One and only God,
Not chairman of the board.

The second commandment tells,
What proper worship is.
Never pray to idols,
Bow down, and all that biz.

God values His Holy Name.
That's what He wants people to see.
And that is just the meaning
Of commandment number three.

A day to rest and worship,
Not a day to be a bore,
To worship and adore:
Yes, commandment number four.

God's family plan is mentioned
In commandment number five.
Honor father and mother,
For this we all should strive.

Each human life within it,
The image of God contains.
You shall do no murder,
Commandment six explains.

Handle your own body
In honor and chastity.
God highly values marriage,
Don't commit adultery.

The eighth commandment has to do
With personal property.
"You shall not steal."
Through it, learn responsibility.

Defend another person's name,
A good name is a treasure.
How we speak of others
Is a moral character measure.

The tenth commandment, the only one
About a heart condition.
You shall not covet, left
Apostle Paul in deep contrition.

And so the Law, a moral mirror,
Exposes all our sin and dross.
Where can we go to cleanse our guilt?
Only at the place of Calvary's Cross.

The only One ever to keep God's Law
Was Jesus Christ, you see.
Christ, the perfect Son of God
Satisfied God's justice for you and me.

Jesus died upon that Cross,
He died for me and you.
He cried, Father, forgive them
For they know not what they do.

How now can I live
With God's Law as a guide?
The way is for the Holy Spirit
To come and live inside.

The First Commandment

I am the LORD your God, who brought you out of the land of Egypt, out of the house of bondage. You shall have no other gods before Me (Exodus 20:2 NKJV).

The 1st Commandment Poem

(God) I am the Lord your God.
    I brought you out of slavery,
    (Therefore) you shall have
    No other gods before Me.

(Man) Is there one God or many?
    This is our question, Lord.
    Are there many so-called gods,
    And You the chairman of the board?

    In Egypt there were many gods
    And now you say there's One.
    Is it really quite so bad
    To worship the god of the sun?

(God) I am the only God there is,
    Oh, children of Israel.
    All these other so-called gods
    Will lead you back to hell.

    I am God, there is no other.
    I have a claim on you.
    I put all the stars in place,
    The moon and the sun, too.

(Man) There are so many functions in the world.
    Now, let's be realistic.
    It seems all people were made
    To be polytheistic.

(God) Polytheism in your heart
    Will produce it in your personality.
    Psychiatry calls it neurosis,
    The Bible, idolatry.

(Man) I have a divided heart.
    It is not very fun.
    My heart's a solitary throne.
    It's made for only One.

    So God, come in and take that place
    And fill my empty hole.
    Take first place in my life,
    Take first place in my soul.

    The Law of the Lord is perfect,
    Yes it converts the soul,
    Reveals Jesus through the Word
    And makes the broken whole.

False Gods

False gods of the ancient world,
Venus, Jupiter, and Mars,
But do we have false gods today?
Tell me, what are ours?

The false gods that we have today
Are taking some gift from God.
Making it central to our lives
Forgetting Him, isn't that odd?

God gave us the gift of sex.
In marriage, ecstasy, and joy,
But if we forget His instructions
And abuse this gift, we'll find it is no toy.

Now science has become a god.
We've pinned our hopes on it for years.
Now it threatens to destroy
We weep our sub-atomic tears.

Sports are good and clean and fun,
As long as they're on the circumference.
But when they become central to life
They can cause quite a disturbance.

Stuff is another god of life.
We live for things money can buy.
Materialism has become our king,
But it can never satisfy.

Life is meant to be a whole.
We cannot serve two masters.
If we allow Jesus to reign supreme,
We'll avert many disasters.

Two Masters

You cannot serve two masters,
But we can try can't we.
And it leaves fragmentation
In my personality.

It causes me neurosis,
According to psychology.
According to the Bible
It is called idolatry.

The human heart was made
For one solitary throne.
Says the God of earth and heaven,
There I must reign alone.

If money is your master
Then you are on your own.
But we're in our heavenly Father's care
When Jesus sits on our heart's throne.

Money is not my master,
To it I will not bow.
The God of heaven, the Lord Jesus Christ,
He is my master now.

Lower Left-Hand Corner

Is
  This
    Where
      You
        Are
          Putting…
God?

Therefore

I Am the Lord your God.
I Am your Creator.
I Am your Deliverer.
I Am your Savior.
I Am your Protector.
I Am your Provider.
I Am yours and you are Mine.
(Therefore) You shall have no other gods before Me.
I Am the Bread of Life.
I Am the Good Shepherd.
I Am the Door.
I Am the True Vine.
I Am the Resurrection and the Life.
I Am the Way, the Truth and the Life.
I Am the Alpha and the Omega.

The Second Commandment

You shall not make for yourself a carved image, or any likeness of anything that is in heaven above, or that is in the earth beneath, or that is in the water under the earth; you shall not bow down to them nor serve them. For I, the LORD your God, am a jealous God, visiting the iniquity of the fathers on the children to the third and fourth generations of those who hate Me, but showing mercy to thousands, to those who love Me and keep My commandments (Exodus 20:4-6 NKJV).

You shall not make for yourself an idol…
(Exodus 20:4a NIV).

Who or What is Your God?

Whatever your heart clings to in size,
Whatever your heart upon relies,
That is your god the Theologian cries.
If it's a small g, God sighs.

What is Idolatry?

The human heart, says the theologian,
Is an idol factory.
But what exactly is this thing
Called idolatry?
It is misplaced allegiance,
Another priority,
That displaces and dethrones
The Blessed Trinity.

Commandments 1 & 2

Commandment number one
Tells us to worship whom.
The one and only triune God
From whom all things come and bloom.

Commandment number two
Tells us to worship how.
To give praise to the invisible God,
And never to an idol bow.

Commandment number one
Tells of God's unity.
Later on we'll learn
God is one in three.

Commandment number two
Tells of God's spirituality.
When He's worshiped in Spirit and Truth,
We'll experience HIS REALITY.

Who He Really is

We have the label Christian,
A cross upon our chest,
Saying the true God lives there,
And knowing our lives are blest.

But have we allowed an idol,
To become our priority?
And kicked the true God off the throne
And bowed to idolatry?

We must not make an idol of anything,
Even something good.
And let God reign upon the throne
As we know we should.

Worshiping that which should be used,
That is idolatry.
Using that which should be worshiped
Is a form of blasphemy.

Is there an idol in your heart?
Can Christ look down and say,
There is a rival for My claim
Over your total personality.

Little children beware of idols.
I'm a God of jealousy,
I tolerate no rival,
No spiritual adultery.

God has a white-hot passion,
Jealous for the good name of His,
Zealous for His covenant with us,
Jealous for us to understand WHO HE REALLY IS.

Jealous?

Is God a jealous God?
Is this really true,
Or overruled by Jesus' teaching,
"You've heard it said of old,
But I say unto you"…?

I Am

Do not make for yourself an idol
Of anything in heaven above.
Not stars or moon or sun,
I Am the Creator, God of love.

Do not make for yourself an idol,
Of anything upon the earth,
Not reptiles, animals or birds
Of nothing they are worth.

Do not make for yourself an idol,
Of anything in the waters below.
I Am not visible at this time,
I come incognito.

You shall not bow down to idols
Or ever worship them.
For whoever worships idols
They, I will condemn.

For I the Lord your God,
I Am a God who is jealous.
I have a white-hot passion
For My people I Am zealous.

I love My people very much,
And so I've put in place,
Both punishments and promises
To lead them in the race.

The punishments are limited
To generations who disobey.
But My promises go on and on
To those on the narrow way.

No image can represent Me,
All idols I shall damn.
Only One can represent Me, Who said,
"Before Abraham was, I Am."

The Only True Picture of God

Where can we find a picture of God,
In the stars and outer space?
No, the only true picture of God we have,
Is in Jesus' lovely face.

Read Matthew, Mark, Luke and John.
Read them all, not just a fraction,
For in those New Testament pages
We see God in action.

He came to earth, was virgin born,
The event, the Incarnation.
God with us, He has skin on,
We observe with fascination.

He cared for people very much,
Preached, taught, healed and cured,
And never once to temptation gave in
Nor by the devil lured.

The sinless One upon the Cross,
For you and me He died.
His death for us atonement made,
With His last breath He sighed.

I commit My Spirit unto You,
Father up above.
It is finished, I've shown Your fame,
God of self-sacrificing love.

The Third Commandment

You shall not take the name of the LORD your God in vain, for the LORD will not hold him guiltless who takes His name in vain (Exodus 20:7 NKJV).

Audience Chamber

Why do people use God's name
For a common oath?
Is it because they are close to Him,
Love Him, or both?

Do people just like to use His name
Time and time again?
Or maybe they don't realize
They take His name in vain.

Do they use His name
As the One upon Whom to call?
Or are they really on speaking
Terms with Him at all?

Do you know anyone who does
Deeply with God commune,
And then turn around,
And His name impune?

Who is close to God that,
Habitually His name misuse,
And carelessly throws it around,
And constantly abuse.

Jesus said, "Our Father in heaven,
Hallowed be Your name."
We are to use His name,
To His eternal fame.

God's name is to be honored,
Worshiped and adored.
God's name is the doorway to
The audience chamber of the Lord.

Oaths

I want you to believe me,
So I think I'll swear,
By God if you don't care,
That will show my sincerity.

When we use God's name in an oath,
We give the impression,
We're making a connection
To our word and to God, yes both.

A Christian takes Christ's name,
But we take His name in vain,
By breaking our word we profane,
So those promises we made are lame.

Jesus said, let your yes be yes,
And let your no be no.
Fulfill your word and don't be slow.
Truthfulness God will bless.

God's Last Name

God says in the third commandment
You shall not misuse My name.
To speak of God with reverence
That should be our aim.

A lot of people seem to think,
That God's last name is damn.
But at this we should recoil,
He is the great I Am.

Moses once spoke to God,
Lord, I'm in quite a jam.
The Israelites will say what is His name?
God said, tell them, I AM WHO I AM.

The great God of the universe,
Shouldn't we be in awe?
The Creator of the cosmos,
Without a single flaw.

He hears and answers all our prayers.
How He does it is out of sight.
We cannot understand it,
He's infinite, we're finite.

Jesus said when you pray
Say, Father, hallowed be Your name.
And we should use our lips
To glorify and proclaim…
                              His Great Name.

In My Name

The disciples were arguing
While they were on the road,
About which one was the greatest
And each other they would goad.

Caught up in a struggle
For personal success,
And hoping that Jesus
Would their desires bless.

What was it you discussed
Among yourselves upon the road?
The Master asked, they looked down,
He sensed their guilty load.

He took a little child
And He sat him in their midst,
And the teaching on greatness
Took quite a little twist.

If anyone desires to be first,
He then shall be the last.
Those power-hungry disciples
I'm sure were quite aghast.

Then He said, to be great
You must be servant of all.
I'm sure they all were silent,
There must have been quite a lull.

Jesus took the child in his arms,
And maybe sat him on His knee,
Whoever receives one of these little ones
In My name, receives Me.

And whoever receives Me,
Receives Him who sent Me.
This is true greatness,
I hope this you will see.

Jesus made Himself
The lowest man of all.
Ministering to needy people, is unto Jesus
And it is the Christian's call.

Uncouth

Do we use God's name inappropriately,
Such as a common word of curse.
Use His name as a common market place,
To commit blasphemy or worse?

The ancient Jews wouldn't even pronounce God's name,
They held it in such awe.
Their Creator, Redeemer, Deliverer,
And the giver of the Law.

Do we ever invoke God's name
With insincerity?
Let your yes be yes and no be no,
That's how our speech should be.

Making promises in God's name
As a cover for the truth,
Lives marked by carelessness, unfaithfulness, perjury
Are very much uncouth.

Being convicted by God's command,
Our life we must now scrutinize.
Come to Him in repentance and faith,
And by His Spirit make us wise.

The Fourth Commandment

Remember the Sabbath day, to keep it holy. Six days you shall labor and do all your work, but the seventh day is the Sabbath of the LORD your God. In it you shall do no work: you, nor your son, nor your daughter, nor your male servant, nor your female servant, nor your cattle, nor your stranger who is within your gates. For in six days the LORD made the heavens and the earth, the sea, and all that is in them, and rested the seventh day. Therefore the LORD blessed the Sabbath day and hallowed it (Exodus 20:8-11 NKJV).

Sunday

Sunday is a special day,
The principle of Sabbath rest,
For rest and worship we obey,
And God's blessings we do attest.

The Lord's day is a special day,
Like John to be in the Spirit.
The Word of God is on display,
In church, that we may hear it.

Sunday is Resurrection day,
When Jesus Christ rose from the dead.
We worship and we shout hooray!
And celebrate the Fountain Head.

Remember the principle of Sabbath day.
It's our sinful nature to forget.
What an awful price that Christ did pay,
On the Cross He cancelled all our debt.

Has Sunday become a holiday
For athletics, the mountains, the movies, the beach,
All for self, recreation and play,
And God's commandment we all breach?

Is Sunday a holy day,
A day set apart to be with God?
To rest this body made of clay
And God's greatness to applaud.

Sunday is the Lord's day.
It's also good for society.
Busyness leaves us in disarray.
We take time for community.

The principle of the Sabbath day,
Was made for the needs of humanity.
A break from life's stress and fray,
To experience love's eternal Trinity.

We remember Jesus on this day.
He is the reason we are blest.
He is the Truth, the Life, the Way.
He is our Eternal Rest.

If we set aside this one day,
To worship the one true God above,
He will refresh our bodies, renew our souls,
Realign our values and restore our love.

Sabbath Time

The church will ring its chime.
The gift of God is time.
The Sabbath day sublime,
This time with God is prime.

God in His fatherhood,
Made all things, called them good.
We spend time with God as we should,
And take a break from our livelihood.

The Sabbath alone for Himself He set apart.
On this day we worship and proclaim how great Thou art.
On this day God renews our body, mind and heart.
The Lord's day is how the week we start.

Six days of work and one day of rest,
This rhythm of time God calls the best.
Where two or three are gathered Christ is manifest.
He heals our hearts and renews our zest.

So all the Lord's day to enroll,
So God can renew us body and soul.
He wants to make us whole,
Conforming us to Christ's image His goal.

The Fifth Commandment

Honor your father and your mother, that your days may be long upon the land which the Lord your God is giving you (Exodus 20:12 NKJV).

Honor

Honor your father and your mother
Does the fifth commandment say,
Esteem them highly, love them,
Respect them and obey.

That your days may be long upon the land
Which the Lord your God is giving you,
The old life of wandering is in the past.
The land He's giving you is new.

Respect for parents reminds us,
That we do not live unto ourselves.
All we have is a gift from God,
So the fifth commandment delves.

Important to God's kingdom,
He loves family stability,
So that it may go well with you,
And indicates the health of society.

God the Creator is the One we worship
Father and mother our human procreators,
They feed, clothe, take care of us
We become their appreciators.

Parents are to be honored, not just obeyed.
This way we acknowledge our dependency.
We obey and honor them,
After all, as children, we live at their residency!

Never Cross a Child

Never cross a child,
The modern guru's teach.
From the parent's rightful rule,
Their children will impeach.

Never thwart him, never punish him,
The child must choose for himself.
Let him become autonomous
The demanding little elf.

Now the child wants to play with a razor
Instead of a harmless toy.
Is it at this time the parents
Direction to employ?

What happens if a youngster behaves
As if the whole world around him revolves?
Selfish and narcissistic,
A little monster evolves.

Do we let a child grow up thinking
He is the center of the universe?
A dim view everyone thinks of this,
And the consequences quite adverse.

Children are self-centered,
It's their natural little quirk.
It's up to parents to teach them
The way the world doesn't work.

Children want to run the world
The way they would like it to run.
But if they always insist on their own way,
They may get hurt, and no longer have any fun.

By nature a child is selfish,
And for a while that's ok.
But it's up to mom and dad to teach them,
That the world doesn't work that way.

Go to church, read the Bible and pray,
An example to set by husband and wife.
That the Holy Spirit may produce His fruit
And through Jesus give children eternal life.

Who's The Boss?

Who is the boss in the home?
Some say it is the man.
But a woman knows how to get her way,
If she's sly she surely can.

Who's in charge in the home,
The woman, the matriarch?
While the man becomes lazy and passive,
His rear on the couch does park.

Who's in charge in the home?
Why here the children rule.
They boss mom and dad around,
And everyone at school.

Who's in charge in the home?
I think it's the TV.
We sit for hours in front of it
Brainwashes the kids, and you and me.

Who's supposed to be in charge of the home?
What does the Bible say?
Mom and dad are at each other's throats,
And the children disobey.

Who's supposed to be in charge of the home?
The Bible says Jesus Christ is supposed to be.
Him we worship and adore,
Before Him we bow the knee.

The Lord Jesus is in charge of the home.
Husband and wife their spirit lifts
Then they submit to one another,
And minister with their particular gifts.

The Lord Jesus is in charge of the home.
Submit to one another, but first to Him.
Children honor, obey mom and dad.
This home, love flows to the brim.

The Lord Jesus is in charge of the home.
Mom and dad mutually care.
Children obey parents in the Lord.
This home, the love of God they share.

The Sixth Commandment

You shall not murder (Exodus 20:13 NKJV).

Murder

You have heard that it was said
To people long ago,
You shall do no murder
With the strike or outward blow.

But Jesus goes much deeper,
Straight into our hearts,
For He knows the place
Where murder really starts.

A relationship is strained,
And words are said to hurt,
Those words caused much damage,
The relationship subvert.

These words wound like arrows
In a person's tender soul.
They burn like acid
And begin to burn a hole.

Resentment starts to build
And we begin to seethe.
Then all kinds of insults
In our minds we can conceive.

Then all those nasty thoughts
Come reeling from our mouth,
And now the relationship
Is really going south.

Insults turn to hatred
And hatred turns to blows.
Now all inhibitions
Our sinful nature overthrows.

Now our angry passion has
Crossed a boundary, went too far.
The scene that's now before us
Is really quite bizarre.

There is now a person
That is lying on the floor.
We are all in shock,
The awful deed we all abhor.

Anger got the best of us,
We struck a person dead.
Now there before us
Innocent blood we have shed.

A voice says, What have you done?
What now have I found?
The voice of your brother's blood
Cries out to Me from the ground.

Now you are subject to judgment.
There's more that I could tell.
Your eternal sentence
Will be in the fire of hell.

Listen to God's warning,
Sin is crouching at your door,
Eagerly waiting to possess you,
And enslave you ever more.

But you must rule over it,
I, God, hold you responsible.
How can I rule my passions?
This is incomprehensible.

The only difference between anger,
And murder is in degree.
We've all broken God's commandment
On this we can agree.

God has mercy and compassion
On one whose heart is rent.
For this reason into the world
His only Son He sent.

There was a murder over yonder
On a hill called Calvary.
There God's Son bore our sins,
In His body on the Tree.

He secured our pardon and forgiveness
In that very hour,
And the promised Holy Spirit
To give us spiritual power.

Power to resist temptation,
To forgive and to love,
This power only comes
With power from above.

To give us spiritual fruit,
In Christian virtues to excel,
To prepare us for heaven,
And escape the flames of hell.

Do Kill Your Enemy (This Way)

Don't kill your enemy,
Love him to death instead.
And you will receive in heaven
A crown of jewels on your head.

Do kill your enemy,
By loving him, and in the end,
He will die as an enemy
And be reborn as a friend.

That's not an easy task,
Jesus never said it would be.
The grace of God will help us
To love our enemy.

It would be impossible,
Except in that we share,
The Spirit of the Holy One
Who helps us love and care.

Be kind and compassionate
To one another too,
Forgiving each other, just as in Christ,
God has forgiven you.

God's Image

Human life is very valuable,
Its word is sanctity,
Because in the image of God
He has created you and me.

Every human life is precious,
In God's image we are made
And if anyone kills another
Of God's judgment be afraid.

So valuable is each human life
God wants us to recognize,
His image in all people
They are precious in His eyes.

Both man and woman
Are in God's image made
And to destroy that image
God requires an accounting paid.

Whoever sheds the blood
Of a woman or a man,
Shall pay with his or her own life
That is God's justice plan.

On the Cross of Calvary
An accounting there was made,
Our sins bore by the Son of God,
God's justice fully paid.

Life and Death

God puts to death
And makes alive!
Without Him
We could not survive.

We need Him
For every breath.
He has control
Of life and death.

Life and death
Are His jurisdiction.
He gives the blessing
And benediction.

He gives the blessing
When life begins.
And the benediction
When life ends.

He made Adam
From the sod.
What gave him life
Was the breath of God.

And man became
A living soul.
Staying close to God
Will keep him whole.

Now with Adam's
Cooperation,
God now performs
An operation.

From Adam's rib
He forms Eve for wife,
To add to each other
Spice to life.

To Adam's great
Elation,
This was a cause
For celebration.

And now God
By delegation,
Gives Adam and Eve
The gift of procreation.

After some time
Adam and Eve fell,
And sin made things
A living hell.

Their first two boys
Were Cain and Able.
Cain was the one
Who was unstable.

Able pleased God,
We hold our breath
Cain's jealousy murdered
His brother to death.

We know this
Was not God's will
But He gives us
Choice and freedom still.

Though Cain was
Not given exemption,
Through Jesus even murderers
Can find redemption.

The Seventh Commandment

You shall not commit adultery (Exodus 20:14 NKJV).

Sexuality

With our bodies we are
To live in sanctity,
In a sex
Saturated society.

You shall not
Commit adultery.
The body is not meant
For sexual immorality.

You are not your own,
You were bought at a price.
Honor God with your body
That would be nice.

Uniting with a prostitute
Is a very bad vice.
Making love with your spouse
Is God's intended paradise.

In marriage a man
And a woman begin to mesh,
The Bible says the two
Will become one flesh.

In this act of intercourse
Their bodies and souls refresh,
A spiritual ministry to each other
That is clean and fresh.

Our bodies are members
Of Christ the Lord.
Into our hearts
The Holy Spirit is poured.

The price He paid for us
We never could afford.
Be true to Jesus and your spouse
And you'll receive His reward.

Adultery and fornication,
They are quite a blight,
And the sinful nature
They can incite.

To God's judgment throne
He will indict,
Never with a
Prostitute unite.

God wants us
To see the light,
In our sexuality
To delight.

So to the man and woman
God does invite,
To marriage where sexual relations
Are good and right.

From fornication
We must flee.
This is called
Indecency.

It is not good
For you or me
And it causes disintegration
In society.

God smiles on sexual relations
Only in heterosexual marriage
Linked with love, unity, procreation
And maybe a baby carriage.

To disobey is a great
Justice miscarriage.
This law of God
We must not disparage.

If anyone has broken this law,
Or maybe you're not sure
On the Cross Jesus bore our sin,
To forgive, restore and make pure.

Shy

Christians have been
Rather shy,
When it comes to sex,
But I don't know why.

We can speak
About sex frankly
We can speak
About sex positively.

God created
Adam as a man.
God created
Eve as a woman.

And a man will
Leave his father
And a man will
Leave his mother.

He will be
United to his wife
This is one of the most
Exciting things in life.

A man and a woman
Become one flesh
Made complementary
So their bodies will mesh.

A man and a woman
Become one,
This is not only necessary,
It is fun!

For procreation
And for pleasure,
Their relationship
They will always treasure.

This one flesh union
In matrimony
Give to all the world
Good testimony.

The pledge before God and others
I am yours and you are mine,
Has the grand approval
Of the Divine.

The 7th Commandment Poem

The seventh commandment is perhaps today,
The most unpopular of them all.
The one under the heaviest fire,
Both philosophical and theological.

The seventh commandment is under assault
By almost every force in society.
They can't believe the commandment says,
"You shall not commit adultery."

Strict

Why is God so strict
About our sexuality?
Maybe because it comes
With such responsibility.

Respect for each
Person's sensitivity,
Establishes the stability
Of the family.

He respects each
Person's individuality
While bringing them
Together in blessed unity.

Marriage suggests permanence
And relationality.
Fornication is forbidden
And may produce unwanted pregnancy.

The commandment is
"You shall not commit adultery."
But sexual intercourse
In marriage is sanctity.

Before marriage
God requires chastity.
After marriage
God requires fidelity.

God will no longer
Tolerate polygamy.
But yes, God smiles
On marital monogamy.

God created
Masculinity.
God created
Femininity.

The man and woman
He made to be complementary.
When they come together
There are not two but three.

Why is God so strict
About our sexuality?
He cares about individuals
And the health of society.

Moral Fences

Today I find it
Quite bizarre
That we don't know where
The moral fences are.

When it comes to
Sexual relations,
God forbids
All fornications.

Fornication refers to
Premarital sex of course.
Adultery is
Extramarital intercourse.

Adultery and fornication
God says are wrong.
Some people say
This is much too strong.

It's as if people
Have never heard,
God's command
In His Holy Word.

Today you are labeled
As a buffoon,
If you wait for sex
On your honeymoon.

But the man and woman
Will be blest,
If they follow God's Word
He knows what's best.

Sexual relations
He does to marriage confine.
For sexual relations
Are His design.

For bonding and pleasure,
Procreation and love,
This is a glorious gift
From God above.

Sex Advice for Husband and Wife

One point of conflict
In this life,
Between a husband
And a wife,
Is the fun and frequency
Of sexual relations,
So when they come together
It's a cause for celebrations.

Men if you would like, to your wife
To be a hitchen',
You need to realize that
Sex begins in the kitchen.
Be helpful, sensitive, romantic,
Let her know you care.
And later on she may run
Her fingers through your hair.

If you want your intercourse
To be let's say, divine,
Then ladies listen to
A little advice of mine.

I've heard it somewhere,
And I know that it's been said,
A man wants an angel in the kitchen
But he likes a devil in bed.

Now don't get too upset
For goodness sake
Most people like angel
And devil's food cake.

When we talk about sex
Some people get riled
But the Bible says the
Marriage bed is undefiled.

Nothing thrills a man more
Than to discover
His wife is an
Enthusiastic lover.

Marriage is where the
Fun is supposed to be,
Not when people commit
Fornication or adultery.

Sex is a perfectly
God-given treasure
For a husband and wife
To enjoy pleasure together.

Happy Marriage

For a happy marriage when the budget is tight,
Well you know what they say,
Don't skimp on excellent food
Or the lingerie!

Wow!

Adam and Eve were originally one flesh.
God performed surgery on Adam.
He took woman from the man.
Now there are two.
God created community.
Hi Eve!
Hi Adam!
Wow!
God Smiles.
(Therefore)
A man shall leave his father and mother,
And be joined to his wife, cling to his wife,
And the two shall become one flesh.
And they were both naked,
The man and his wife,
And were not ashamed.
Not ashamed.
Wow!
To become again one flesh is figurative language
For the physical act of sexual union,
Intended by God to take place only
Within marriage.
The unity of husband and wife
Is similar
To the unity of Christ and the Church.
The Apostle Paul says,
This is a great mystery!
This is a glorious mystery!
Wow!

The Eighth Commandment

You shall not steal (Exodus 20:15 NKJV).

The 8th Commandment Poem

The eighth commandment protects us,
It says you shall not steal.
From liars, cheaters and swindlers,
And those who falsely deal.

You shall not cheat your neighbor,
Nor from him shall you rob.
For God is a God of justice,
For the oppressed His heart does throb.

Dignity

No civilization can long survive
Without respect for personal property.
Which assumes the right
To individual liberty.

Property rights are one
Vital expression of personal dignity,
And the worth of each person
Which gives each life quality.

Thief

I went to the city pool for my summer job.
It was a hot day so there was a mob.
I sat up in the lifeguard chair,
And I spotted a little girl with shoulder-length-red hair.
She was only about the age of five,
And no mom or dad around to supervise.
It was on a day in July at the city pool,
It was getting hotter, people wanted to be cool.
All kinds of people laid their towels on the deck,
With a carefree attitude, let's go swimming, what the heck.
But the little red-haired girl in her one-piece, lime-green suit,
Went around from towel to towel, she really was kind of cute.
And as she sneakily went around and lifted up a towel,
The little girl in the lime-green suit was as silent as an owl.
But her ear was ever wary of the noise of coins that ring,
And when she found some money, her eyes they went cha ching!
When she had a handful of loot that was not her own,
She would skip over to the concession stand and buy herself a snow cone.
The little red-haired girl in the lime-green suit was crafty for her size.
It's really too bad her mom and dad weren't around to supervise.
For though she got what she wanted and her thirst got some relief,
The little red-haired girl in the lime-green suit was learning to be a thief.

The Ninth Commandment

You shall not bear false witness against your neighbor (Exodus 20:16 NKJV).

The Ways We Lie

The ways we lie are many.
We can go about and tell,
We can spread a lie by gossip,
A tongue set on fire by hell.

We can live a lie, that's hardship,
An image we try to sell,
A life that doesn't back up our word,
Though false words with vigor we yell.

But the Spirit of God touches us
And convicts us at the heart's citadel.
For our lies Jesus' atonement made
Through His broken body and many a red blood cell.

The Cure for Lying

For lying there is a cure,
So that you won't be impure.
Tell the truth right away
And do not delay,
So that you might become mature.

Sorry Mom for Lying

Is there a cure for lying?
I try and keep on trying,
To tell the truth,
While I'm still in my youth,
And to keep my mom from crying.

The Truth and a Lie

What is the difference between the truth and a lie?
I can't tell the difference. I don't know why.
For so long I've been such a liar,
With lies my tongue is set on fire.
I know that this is not ok,
But I have an image to portray.
These lies originate in my mind to start,
To cover my cowardly lying heart.
I want to break this awful habit.
Sometimes I don't think I'll make it.
But if Jesus bears my lies with His nailed feet,
And fills me with the *Paraclete,
Then courage I will have, the truth to face,
Since Jesus on the Cross took my place,
…and bore my disgrace.

*Note: Paraclete-the Holy Spirit, the One who comes alongside to help.

Court Justice

Clever lawyers the truth they twist,
And confuse an eyewitness.
A false witness is then exalted,
Now the truth is catapulted.
Much dust is thrown up in the air!
Can the trial even now be fair?
Now the trial comes to a close.
What's the truth? No one knows.

The Human Heart

What is the truth of the human heart?
Where shall we go, or look, or start?
As all of history I look across,
One thing stands out, it is the Cross.

The Cross upon which Jesus died,
Where he bled and hung, was crucified.
He bore our sins upon that Tree,
Where He died for you and me.

I contemplate, I realize,
My heart, it is a fraud.
I am bad enough to crucify
The very Son of God.

God has always known,
The badness of our heart,
If we admit, confess, repent of it
He'll give us a new start.

And by the Holy Spirit
He'll cleanse the human heart.

Words

We cannot recapture
Our words once they have flown.
So we must be careful
What kind of message we have sown.

Words can ruin very much
A person's reputation.
And that is so unlike
The man called the Galilean.

The tongue with words
Can blast a life,
And cause a person
So much strife.

Harmful words can damage
A person's effectiveness,
And that person's spirit
Could very much depress.

The tongue can wreak much havoc,
It is a world of fire,
When harmful words they come
From the mouth of a liar.

Reputation

God is a God of holy truth.
To bear false witness is uncouth.
Especially concerning relationships,
To be careful how we use our lips.
The right to enjoy a good reputation,
Is a cause for celebration.
Untarnished by other people's lies,
On a good name we can capitalize.
And live in a society,
That relieves our anxiety.
Your reputation ought be safe with me.
God says, this is a necessity.

Respectable Christians

Some of the most respectable Christians,
Who would never dream of murder or theft,
Start right upon the narrow way
Then make a sharp turn left.

Did you hear about so and so,
Oh, it's such a juicy thing.
And these most respectable Christians
Engage in the deadly sin of gossiping.

Now we all live in community,
We want to be informed and smart.
But before we pass these tidbits on,
Is it true? What's the motive of the heart?

Now we would look down on drunkenness,
And those who over drink the ale.
But do we examine our own hearts
Before we pass on the deadly tale?

Some of the most respectable Christians
Self-righteously spread this deadly leaven,
And that is the very reason
They may be barred from heaven.

But if these most respectable Christians,
Repent of this genuine sin,
And are truly sorry for the damage they've done,
Christ will forgive them again.

The Living Lie

Jesus' road to the Cross
Was filled with the living liar,
Let me name several,
To be a testifier.

The scribes claimed to have knowledge
That they did not possess.
The Pharisees were not,
But they claimed righteousness.

The false witnesses who told stories,
Of things they had not seen or heard,
Even the mock trial leaders
Knew their lies were quite absurd.

Judas whose loving gesture
Was on Jesus' cheek a kiss,
And that most heinous sin,
Sent him to the abyss.

"What is truth?" asked Pilate,
Trying to sound so smart,
To cover up and disguise
His cowardly lying heart.

But what about you and me,
Have we ever lied?
And projected a false image
Because of our selfish pride.

Surely God desires
Truth in our inner parts.
God teach us wisdom in the secret place,
And come and cleanse our hearts.

God Can and Can't

Yes, God is all powerful,
But some things He can't even do.
So I thought I'd take a minute
To share with you a few.

God cannot share His glory
For He is God alone.
God cannot violate human freedom,
Though Christ on the Cross did our sin atone.

God cannot tolerate sin,
For He is too holy and pure within.
And finally I'd like to amplify
He is a God of truth, He cannot tell a lie.

Ain't

Many a Christian person,
Who would never ever kill
Let their mouths run over,
And tall tales over-spill.

She would never ever think
To commit adultery
But let some malicious gossip come,
And her lips are loose and free.

Many Christians would never
From someone's possessions steal,
But to pass on a juicy story we've heard,
It does have some appeal.

Yes, when we are tearing others down,
Right down to the letter,
Somehow it makes us feel so good,
Like we are so much better.

Yes, when we tale bear and gossip,
We can even feel like a saint,
But when we ruin others' reputations,
It might mean that we ain't.

Fly Catcher

A man sat there with his
Mouth catching flies,
As another man confessed to him
All of his lies.
The first man had
The wide open eyes,
And then he began
To realize
That the other guy was coming clean,
Coming as clean as you can,
And was on his way to becoming
A much, much better man.

Ouch

A man lay on a psychologist's couch,
To get through the layers of his deceitful ways,
The psychologist probed to get a psychic ouch,
But in his thick denial he stays.

He preferred to stay in his delusion.
He did not like the shrink's intrusion.
And so he began to defend
His dysfunctional ways to the end.

Between the patient and the shrink
There became quite a schism,
Because of the patient's hair trigger,
Defense mechanism.

But then the man began to cry
And admit that he had been living a lie.
The man had a deceitful heart.
How could he get a new start?

As the man lay on the psychologist's couch,
The psychologist had his questioning ways,
Which finally got the psychic ouch.
Tears flowed as the man there lays.

God now says when you get real,
You and I will make a deal.
There is One who bore your sin,
Died, was buried, and rose again.

A broken and a contrite heart
God will not despise.
He will give you a new start.
This, the Spirit helps us realize.

The Tenth Commandment

You shall not covet your neighbor's house; you shall not covet your neighbor's wife, nor his male servant, nor his female servant, nor his ox, nor his donkey, nor anything that is your neighbor's (Exodus 20:17 NKJV).

Covetousness

It was the summer before I started eighth grade.
I had mowed yards for almost two summers
To get enough money to buy my dream bicycle,
An orange Varsity Schwinn ten-speed bicycle.
I finally went up to the bike shop and bought it.
I was so happy and content and proud
To have such a nice bicycle,
For everyone to see my new bicycle,
And that I had paid for it myself.
I was so happy and content.
Then,
About a week later,
My friend and neighbor, Kyle rode up
With his brand-spanking new bicycle,
Light blue (the newest color)
Schwinn Super Sport (two grades above mine)
Twelve-speed (two gears more than mine)
Toe clips for the pedals (for power going up and down)
The bike was made of aluminum (that means his bicycle was lighter and faster than mine)
And his parents bought it for him!
I was in awe.
It was a really nice bicycle.
His bicycle was newer, nicer, faster and cooler than mine.
I was happy for him (sort of…)
But I became depressed and sad.
His bike was better than the one I had.
What caused me to be unhappy?
Covetousness!
What is covetousness?

It is a mirage.
It is a defect in my human heart.
It produces wretchedness in me.
Why?
Because covetousness fixed my gaze
On something I did not have,
So that I did not praise God and thank God
For what I did have.
I still liked my orange Varsity Schwinn ten-speed bicycle.
But why couldn't I have had
The best bicycle on the block for a little
While longer?
Covetousness!

The Tenth Commandment Poem

You shall not covet your neighbor's house.
You shall not covet your neighbor's spouse.
You shall not covet your neighbor's manservant.
You shall not covet your neighbor's maidservant.
You shall not covet your neighbor's donkey or ox,
For that would be unorthodox.
You shall not covet anything that belongs to your Neighbor.
Be content.
I won't belabor.

Law and Gospel

But now, by dying to what once bound us, we have been released from the law so that we serve in the new way of the Spirit, and not in the old way of the written code (Romans 7:6 NIV).

Grace and Truth

For the Law was given through Moses,
Grace and truth are Jesus' roses.
We must distinguish between the Law, its place,
And that which came through Christ, His grace.
It must make the devil much amused
To see Christians so confused.
Commandment one teaches, God wants our sincere trust,
To fear Him above all, this is a must.
We are like children, punished by our Father above,
And yet we are still confident in our Father's love.
The commandment is good and must be obeyed,
But have we kept it perfectly? No, all have strayed.
Except for Christ, everyone is a sinner.
In the Father's eyes, He is the winner.
Christ comes to us now and says however,
I have shed my blood for you forever.
My blood cries out on your behalf.
I trust in Him, I weep, I laugh!
Out of His kindness and His grace,
He brings redemption that lights up my face.
The commandments show my sin, I'm lost.
Christ brings the forgiveness of sins, to us no cost.

Law and Gospel

If we say we are saved by faith alone,
Then where does the Law fit in?
If we can't be saved by keeping the Law,
Then how can salvation be lost by sin?

Does the Christian live above the Law?
Like, I'm not under Law, but under grace?
What's the relationship between Law and faith,
The commandments of God and the Gospel's place?

Love and Law are not incompatible.
Love needs Law to guide it.
Love is the fulfillment of the Law
In the sense that love obeys it.

We can obey God's commands,
With the Holy Spirit's aid.
God's commands can be fulfilled.
We should strive they be obeyed.

We have an Advocate with the Father,
If we should stumble and fall.
He will forgive, renew and cleanse.
He is the greatest One of all.

God's Offer

What does the Gospel offer
To my rebellion and resistance?
Christ offers full pardon, forgiveness
And to obey, supernatural assistance.

The Purpose of God's Law

What is the purpose of the Law?
To show we are sinners one and all.
And to send us to Jesus to be justified.
He sends us back to the Law to be a guide.

The Cross as a Tree

Jesus Christ died
For you and me
Nailed to a Cross,
Or hanged on a Tree?

Jesus bore in our place
The curse of the broken Law.
Hanged on a Tree is a statement
That is profoundly theological.

The Law pronounces judgment
On anyone who breaks it.
On the Cross, on the Tree,
For us, Christ did take it.

Peter and Paul are at one in seeing
The Cross as a Tree, the place of a curse.
The innocent suffering Savior
There did our sins disperse.

Four Limericks on Law and Grace

The commandments begin in grace,
For the entire human race.
The commandments are good,
To obey as we should,
Makes the world a wonderful place.

The commandments we cannot obey,
Our sinful nature to stay.
We need a new heart,
To get a new start,
To be with God ok.

Jesus died on the Cross
To take away all of our dross.
To take all our sin,
And come dwell within,
We surrender, He's our leader, our boss.

The Ten Commandments bring conviction,
And to the heart, deep contrition.
Till at the Cross we find grace,
In Jesus' pardoning face,
Giving us a new heart condition.

Exodus and John

For the law was given through Moses,
But grace and truth came through Jesus Christ (John 1:17 NKJV).

Exodus

The book of Exodus
Is a book about redemption.
The redeemed now, however,
Must have a new intention.

The ones redeemed must consecrate
Their wills to their Master.
If not, it will only lead
To personal and national disaster.

Consecrated to God's service
And submitting to His control,
And not acting according
To the latest opinion poll.

God gave the Ten Commandments
And all the moral Law,
So people would strive to live for God
And He be their all in all.

If one broke the moral Law
Would there be provision?
The ceremonial law followed so
A violator could be assured he's forgiven.

All Old Testament types and shadows,
Jesus Christ fulfills them all.
Christ's pardon is available to everyone,
This does my heart enthrall!

Two Mountains

Two mountains are within my view,
One is old, the other new.
One has the capacity to undo.
The other the power to renew.

The old mountain is called Mount Sinai,
Where the standards given are very high.
I fall so short, it makes me cry.
In exasperation, I sigh.

The new one is called Mount Calvary,
Where Jesus bore our sins on a Tree.
He suffered there for you and me,
So the face of God we could one day see.

Mount Sinai with all its horrors fall,
Thundered forth God's mighty Law.
Mount Calvary made possible the Gospel call,
A meeting place between God and sinners all.

Moses

Man of God
Often felt inadequate because of a
Speech impediment, but with God's help led the
Exodus of the Israelites from Egypt to Mount
Sinai where God gave the Ten Commandments.

Mount Sinai

Moses led the Israelites
Out of Egypt to Mount Sinai where God gave the Law.
Unbelieving,
Nobody obeyed.
They, like we, broke all of God's Ten Commandments.

So, God sent His only begotten Son by the
Incarnation, that whoever believes in Him should
Not perish, but have everlasting life.
As Moses lifted up the serpent in the wilderness, even so must the Son of Man be lifted up, that whoever believes
In Him should not perish but have eternal life.

The Ten Commandments

Trinity: Father, Son & Holy Spirit; one God, three persons.
Hear, O Israel: The Lord our God, the Lord is one!
Esteem them highly!

Teach them diligently to your children!
Exodus Chapter 20
Never ignore them!

Conviction, contrition, come to Jesus, come Holy Spirit.
Observe them in the land that I am giving you.
Mount Sinai
Moses
Always keep all My commandments.
Nailed to the cross was Jesus, because we broke God's commands.
Deuteronomy Chapters 5 & 6,
Meditate on them night and day.
Enjoy the blessings of obedience.
Not is a boundary.
That it might be well with them and with their children forever.
Spirit empowered obedience.

Decalogue

Determine to obey.
Establish them in your heart.
Commandments to obey.
Again obey, I say.
Live in covenant relationship with God.
Obey them so that it may be well with you.
Great is your reward in earth and heaven.
Unless you disobey.
Everything by grace, trust and obey.

The Trinitarian Blessing

The grace of the Lord Jesus Christ,
And the love of God, and the fellowship
Of the Holy Spirit to be with you all (2 Corinthians 13:14 NKJV).

The Trinity

God in three persons
The blessed Trinity.
And yet three persons
Are one in blessed unity.

Some people think
This doctrine is rather odd,
But the Bible is where
We get our teaching about God.

One plus one plus one equals three.
One times one times one equals one.
The Bible teaches that God
Is Father, Spirit, Son.

God is one and God is three,
Father, Son and Holy Spirit,
The Bible teaches this doctrine
Come now all and hear it.

The grace, mercy and love of the Father,
The sacrificial death of the Son,
The cleansing and empowerment of the Holy Spirit
Is how our salvation is won.

Love then is eternal
Between the One in Three.
They each love each other
And overflows to you and me.

Father, Son and Holy Spirit,
He loves all of creation
Especially people in His image
Of every tribe and tongue and nation.

Our God is a social God
Each one loves the other,
And binds believers in one spirit.
They love as sister, brother.

Jesus said, "A new command I give to you:
Love one another.
As I have loved you,
So you must love one another."

Yes, God is a Trinity
And God is from above
The most striking attribute of this triune God
Is that God is love.

God's Will

Your kingdom come,
Your will be done
On earth as it is in heaven (Matthew 6:10 NKJV).

My Will and God's Will

God's will, is it alien,
Or is His will imposed?
Or is it my native air
Which in my blood warmer flows?

The will of God is our highest interest.
When I find His will, I find my own.
Yes, His will is the native air,
Affects my nerves, my blood and bone.

Every organ in my body
Functions better under His control.
Let fear, selfishness or resentments reign,
They function badly and send me on a roll.

When I make Jesus central
It is then I am fulfilled
All other things circumference
At my center I am stilled.

Oh, what a destiny I have
Conforming to the image of His Son,
God's will is not alien.
It's my destiny and it is fun!
              Most of the time.

Sorry, Thank you, Please

How can I ask Jesus
To come into my life
So He can come and take away
My guilt and sin and strife.

There is a little prayer,
It can be said with ease,
A short, sincere prayer called
Sorry, thank you, please.

Sorry, heavenly Father
For the things that I've done wrong.
The guilt I feel is painful
And the power of sin is strong.

Thank you, Lord Jesus Christ
For dying on the Cross for me,
The Son of God paying the ransom price
To pardon and set me free.

Please, crucified and risen Savior
Come in, be my soul carer.
By Your Spirit remake, renew,
That I may be Your image bearer.

Would you like to see your manuscript become a book?

If you are interested in becoming a PublishAmerica author, please submit your manuscript for possible publication to us at:

acquisitions@publishamerica.com

You may also mail in your manuscript to:

**PublishAmerica
PO Box 151
Frederick, MD 21705**

www.publishamerica.com

PublishAmerica

CPSIA information can be obtained at www.ICGtesting.com
Printed in the USA
BVOW012240081211

277951BV00001B/2/P